GOLDEN RETRIEVERS

A BOOK OF 21 POSTCARDS

W9-CDI-719

BROWNTROUT PUBLISHERS
SAN FRANCISCO • CALIFORNIA

BROWNTROUT PUBLISHERS

P. O. BOX 280070
SAN FRANCISCO • CALIFORNIA 94128-0070
800 938 7688

ISBN: 1-56313-918-9
TITLE: 918

BROWNTROUT publishes a large line of calendars, photographic books, and postcard books.
Please write for more information.

Printed in Korea

GOLDEN RETRIEVERS

"The dog represents all that is best in man." —ÉTIENNE CHARLET

BROWNTROUT PUBLISHERS • SAN FRANCISCO, CALIFORNIA

GOLDEN RETRIEVERS

"Don't keep your dog always on a leash
if you want him to be attached to you." —A. Willemetz

PUBLISHED BY BROWNTROUT • SAN FRANCISCO, CALIFORNIA

GOLDEN RETRIEVERS

"A dog will never forget the crumb thou gavest him." —SA'DI

PUBLISHED BY BROWNTROUT • SAN FRANCISCO, CALIFORNIA

GOLDEN RETRIEVERS

"I would rather see a portrait of a dog that I know,
than all the allegorical paintings in the world."   –SAMUEL JOHNSON

PUBLISHED BY BROWNTROUT • SAN FRANCISCO, CALIFORNIA

GOLDEN RETRIEVERS

"A good dog deserves a good bone." —Ben Johnson

PUBLISHED BY BROWNTROUT • SAN FRANCISCO, CALIFORNIA

GOLDEN RETRIEVERS

"Histories are more full of examples of fidelity of dogs than of friends."
—ALEXANDER POPE

PUBLISHED BY BROWNTROUT • SAN FRANCISCO, CALIFORNIA

GOLDEN RETRIEVERS

"Here, gentlemen, a dog teaches us a lesson in humanity."

—NAPOLEON BONAPARTE

PUBLISHED BY BROWNTROUT • SAN FRANCISCO, CALIFORNIA

GOLDEN RETRIEVERS

"I agree with Agassiz that dogs possess something very like a conscience."
— CHARLES DARWIN

PUBLISHED BY BROWNTROUT • SAN FRANCISCO, CALIFORNIA

GOLDEN RETRIEVERS

"The Almighty, who gave the dog to be the companion of our pleasures and toils, hath invested him with a nature noble and incapable of deceit."
— Sir Walter Scott

PUBLISHED BY BROWNTROUT • SAN FRANCISCO, CALIFORNIA

GOLDEN RETRIEVERS

"The more I see of men, the more I admire dogs." —MADAME DE SÉVIGNÉ

PUBLISHED BY BROWNTROUT • SAN FRANCISCO, CALIFORNIA

GOLDEN RETRIEVERS

"Dogs are indeed the most affectionate,
and amiable animals of the whole brute creation." —EDMUND BURKE

PUBLISHED BY BROWNTROUT • SAN FRANCISCO, CALIFORNIA

GOLDEN RETRIEVERS

"In the concurring opinion of the wise, a dog, thankful for his food,
is more worthy than a human being who is devoid of gratitude." —SA'DI

PUBLISHED BY BROWNTROUT • SAN FRANCISCO, CALIFORNIA

GOLDEN RETRIEVERS

"Dog. A kind of additional or subsidiary deity designed
to catch the overflow and surplus of the world's worship."

— AMBROSE BIERCE

PUBLISHED BY BROWNTROUT • SAN FRANCISCO, CALIFORNIA

GOLDEN RETRIEVERS

"Qui me amat, amat et canum meum." —St. Bernard

PUBLISHED BY BROWNTROUT • SAN FRANCISCO, CALIFORNIA

GOLDEN RETRIEVERS

"The dog was created specially for children. He is the god of frolic."
— HENRY WARD BEECHER

PUBLISHED BY BROWNTROUT • SAN FRANCISCO, CALIFORNIA

GOLDEN RETRIEVERS

"The great pleasure of a dog is that you may make a fool of yourself with him and not only will he not scold you, but he will make a fool of himself too."

—SAMUEL BUTLER

PUBLISHED BY BROWNTROUT • SAN FRANCISCO, CALIFORNIA

GOLDEN RETRIEVERS

"The poor dog, in life the firmest friend
The first to welcome, foremost to defend."
—LORD BYRON

PUBLISHED BY BROWNTROUT • SAN FRANCISCO, CALIFORNIA

GOLDEN RETRIEVERS

"They are better than human beings, because they know but do not tell."
—EMILY DICKINSON

PUBLISHED BY BROWNTROUT • SAN FRANCISCO, CALIFORNIA

GOLDEN RETRIEVERS

"…he will be our friend for always and always and always."

—RUDYARD KIPLING

PUBLISHED BY BROWNTROUT • SAN FRANCISCO, CALIFORNIA

GOLDEN RETRIEVERS

" 'Tis sweet to know there is an eye will mark
Our coming and look brighter when we come." —LORD BYRON

PUBLISHED BY BROWNTROUT • SAN FRANCISCO, CALIFORNIA

GOLDEN RETRIEVERS

"Loving friend, the gift of one
Who her own true faith has run
Through thy lower nature,
Be my benediction said
With my hand upon thy head,
Gentle fellow-creature!"

—Elizabeth Barrett Browning

PUBLISHED BY BROWNTROUT • SAN FRANCISCO, CALIFORNIA